PREHISTORIC WORLD

TRIASSIC LIFE

Dougal Dixon

Copyright © 2006 *ticktock* Entertainment Ltd. First published in Great Britain by ticktock Media Ltd.,
Unit 2, Orchard Business Centre, North Farm Road, Tunbridge Wells, Kent TN2 3XF, Great Britain.

A CIP catalogue record for this book is available from the British Library.

ISBN 1 84696 033 9

Printed in China

CONTENTS

INTRODUCTION

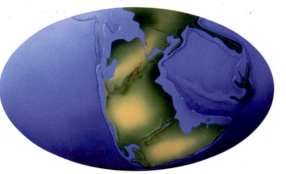

This map shows how the Earth looked in the Triassic Period. All of the continents were grouped into one mass of land.

This map shows how the Earth looks today. See how different it is! The continents have split up and moved around.

Prehistoric World is a series of six books about the evolution of animals.

The Earth's history is divided into sections called periods. These periods last millions of years. Each book in this series looks at the most important periods in prehistory.

This book looks at the Triassic Period, a time when reptiles were common in the seas, the sky and on the land. This is when the first dinosaurs, and the ancestors of the mammals, started to evolve.

PREHISTORIC WORLD TIMELINE

Use this timeline to trace prehistoric life. It shows how simple creatures evolved into more different kinds. This took millions and millions of years. That is what MYA stands for – millions of years ago.

	BOOK	PERIOD	
CENOZOIC ERA	**THE ICE AGE**	1.75 MYA to now QUATERNARY	This is a period of ice ages and mammals. Our direct relatives, Homo sapiens, also appear.
	ANCIENT MAMMALS	65 to 1.75 MYA TERTIARY	Giant mammals and huge, hunting birds appear in this period. Our first human relatives also start to evolve.
MESOZOIC ERA	**CRETACEOUS LIFE**	135 to 65 MYA CRETACEOUS	Huge dinosaurs evolve. They all die by the end of this period.
	JURASSIC LIFE	203 to 135 MYA JURASSIC	Large and small dinosaurs and flying creatures develop.
	TRIASSIC LIFE	250 to 203 MYA TRIASSIC	The 'Age of Dinosaurs' begins. Mammals also start to appear.
PALAEOZOIC ERA	**EARLY LIFE**	295 to 250 MYA PERMIAN	Sail-backed reptiles start to appear.
		355 to 295 MYA CARBONIFEROUS	The first reptiles appear and tropical forests develop.
		410 to 355 MYA DEVONIAN	Bony fish evolve. Trees and insects appear.
		435 to 410 MYA SILURIAN	Fish with jaws develop and land creatures appear.
		500 to 435 MYA ORDOVICIAN	Primitive fishes, trilobites, shellfish and plants evolve.
		540 to 500 MYA CAMBRIAN	First animals with skeletons appear.

SEPHODERMA

By the time of the Triassic Period, there were all kinds of animals living on land. There were also many that returned to the sea and found it easier to live there. The placodonts were a group of reptiles that lived in the sea and ate shellfish. *Psephoderma* had a long, pointed snout and strong jaws. It was ideally adapted for picking shellfish off reefs and crushing them with its broad teeth.

Psephoderma

Psephoderma had a shell on its back and looked rather like a turtle. You can see the shell in this fossil. However, *Psephoderma* was not closely related to the turtles. It evolved a similar shape and shell because it had a similar lifestyle.

Placochelys

Henodus

NAME: *Psephoderma* (rough skin)

PRONOUNCED: sef-oh-der-ma

GROUP: Placodont – a group of swimming shellfish-eaters

WHERE IT LIVED: The seas around Southern Europe

WHEN IT LIVED: Late Triassic Period (223 to 209 million years ago)

LENGTH: 1.5 metres

SPECIAL FEATURES: Turtle-like shell on the back, and another over the hips

FOOD: Shellfish

MAIN ENEMY: Other big swimming reptiles and shark-like fish

DID YOU KNOW?: Not all placodonts had shells. Some looked like giant newts. One relative, *Placodus*, was 2 metres long.

The placodonts in this picture all had armoured backs. Their shells would have protected them from the other sea-living reptiles of the time – some of which were much bigger and fiercer.

NOTHOSAURUS

Nothosaurus was one of the earliest sea-living reptilian hunters. Its feet were webbed, like those of a seal, and it had quite a long neck and long toothy jaws – just right for snatching at fish. It had a long tail to help it to swim. Even though *Nothosaurus* spent most of its time in the water, it had to come to the surface to breathe.

Ceresiosaurus

There were several types of nothosaur. *Lariosaurus* was one of the smallest, about 60 cm long. *Ceresiosaurus* and *Nothosaurus* were bigger and better adapted to life in the sea. They had long necks that made it easier to catch fish, and feet that were used like paddles.

Lariosaurus

Nothosaurus

Fossils of nothosaurs – the group to which *Nothosaurus* belonged – have been found all over the world. *Nothosaurus* was the most common and widespread of them.

SHONISAURUS

Among the reptiles that returned to the sea, probably the most famous are the ichthyosaurs – the 'fish-lizards'. These were so well adapted to living in the sea that they could not have spent any time on land. Some of the earliest forms, like *Shonisaurus* were truly enormous – truly whale-sized.

Shonisaurus was the biggest sea animal of the Triassic Period. One species, *Shonisaurus sikanniensis*, was 21 metres long. Its fossil was found in a remote river bank in Canada.

ANIMAL
FACTFILE

NAME: *Shonisaurus* (lizard from the Shoshone Mountains, Nevada, USA)

PRONOUNCED: shon-ee-sawr-us

GROUP: Ichthyosaur — the fish-lizards

WHERE IT LIVED: The sea which covered parts of the USA and Canada in Triassic times

WHEN IT LIVED: Late Triassic Period (235 to 223 million years ago)

LENGTH: 15 metres

SPECIAL FEATURES: Its size! It was the biggest ichthyosaur known

FOOD: Fish and sea-going invertebrates, like ammonites

MAIN ENEMY: None

DID YOU KNOW?: Scientists think that *Shonisaurus* only had teeth when it was young. Adults were toothless.

This fossil shows a typical ichthyosaur. These reptiles were strong swimmers with streamlined bodies that enabled them to slide effortlessly through the water. The large paddles were actually fingers that had become joined together.

EUDIMORPHODON

Towards the end of the Triassic Period the reptiles mastered the skill of flying. Until then there had been a few lizard-like reptiles that were able to glide for long distances. But now the pterosaurs appeared – reptiles that could fly by flapping their wings like birds. *Eudimorphodon* was one of the first of the pterosaurs.

The pointed front teeth of *Eudimorphodon* were ideal for catching fish as it flew low over the surface of quiet lagoons. The smaller teeth at the back of the mouth would have gripped the slippery prey firmly while it was taken back to land to be eaten.

Like other pterosaurs, *Eudimorphodon* had wings that were supported by a single, long fourth finger. It also had a long stiff tail that it used for steering.

ANIMAL FACTFILE

NAME: *Eudimorphodon* (with two very differently shaped teeth)

PRONOUNCED: you-dee-morf-oh-don

GROUP: Pterosaur – the flying reptiles

WHERE IT LIVED: Italy

WHEN IT LIVED: Late Triassic Period (235 to 208 million years ago)

BODY LENGTH: 0.6 metres

WINGSPAN: 1 metre

SPECIAL FEATURES: Two different types of teeth

FOOD: Fish

MAIN ENEMY: Big fish and big reptiles

DID YOU KNOW?: One fossil of a close relative, *Preondactylus,* was found as a bundle of bones coughed up by a fish that had eaten it over 200 million years ago.

13

ESMATOSUCHUS

Before the dinosaurs evolved, the largest land animals were relatives of today's crocodiles. Some of these animals, like *Desmatosuchus*, were actually plant-eaters. They fed on ferns and other low-growing vegetation. These plants could be found near the oases of the desert landscapes of the time.

The back of *Desmatosuchus* was covered in rows of armour plates. Long spikes curved outwards from the shoulders and neck, helping to protect it against fierce predators such as the meat-eating, land-living crocodiles.

ANIMAL
FACTFILE

NAME: *Desmatosuchus* (link crocodile)

PRONOUNCED: des-mat-oh-sue-kus

GROUP: Aetosaur – a group of plant-eating crocodiles

WHERE IT LIVED: Arizona, Texas

WHEN IT LIVED: Late Triassic Period (233 to 223 million years ago)

LENGTH: 4.8 metres

SPECIAL FEATURES: Long spines on the shoulders for protection

FOOD: Low-growing plants

MAIN ENEMY: Carnivorous land-living crocodiles

DID YOU KNOW?: *Desmatosuchus* was a very early member of the plant-eating crocodile group.

Desmatosuchus had weak, blunt teeth and a short snout. Its head was held close to the ground where the vegetation grew.

RIZONASAURUS

The fiercest meat-eaters in Triassic times were big land-living crocodiles like *Arizonasaurus*. They did not crawl, like modern crocodiles, but walked on straight legs, like dogs. They prowled around the desert landscapes hunting the big plant-eating reptiles that lived in the oases of the time.

The sail may have kept *Arizonasaurus* warm, by taking in heat from the Sun in the chilly mornings. This would have made it more active than its slow-moving prey, and would have helped it to hunt.

The first fossils of *Arizonasaurus* were found in 1947, but the scientists of the time thought they were just dinosaur bones. It was not until 2000 that it was realised the fossils came from a type of crocodile, not a dinosaur. The new animal was named *Arizonasaurus*.

ANIMAL FACTFILE

NAME: *Arizonasaurus* (lizard from Arizona)

PRONOUNCED: a-riz-oh-na-sawr-us

GROUP: Rauisuchian — a group of land-living crocodiles

WHERE IT LIVED: Arizona

WHEN IT LIVED: Middle Triassic Period (240 to 230 million years ago)

LENGTH: 3 metres

SPECIAL FEATURES: Tall sail on its back

FOOD: Plant-eating reptiles

MAIN ENEMY: Bigger land-living crocodiles

DID YOU KNOW?: *Arizonasaurus* looked rather like *Dimetrodon*, an earlier reptile with a sail on its back. In fact, these two reptiles are not closely related. They look the same because their lifestyles were similar.

EORAPTOR

In late Triassic times, many of the big land animals were crocodile relatives and other reptiles. The first dinosaurs were really quite small. *Eoraptor* was only the size of a fox, but it was an ancestor of the huge and magnificent dinosaurs to come.

This copy of an *Eoraptor* skull shows its long jaws and sharp teeth, just like those of later meat-eating dinosaurs. *Eoraptor* was also the same general shape as later predators. Its small body was carried on two strong hind legs. The arms were smaller with grasping fingers and its neck was long and flexible. A long heavy tail helped the dinosaur to balance.

ANIMAL
FACTFILE

NAME: *Eoraptor* (early hunter)

PRONOUNCED: ee-oh-rap-tor

GROUP: Theropod dinosaur

WHERE IT LIVED: Patagonia in South America

WHEN IT LIVED: Late Triassic Period (228 million years ago)

LENGTH: 1 metre

SPECIAL FEATURES: The earliest dinosaur known

FOOD: Small animals and insects

MAIN ENEMY: Big land-living crocodiles

DID YOU KNOW?: Later meat-eating dinosaurs had three, or even two, fingers on the hand. Like its ancestors, *Eoraptor* still had five, although two of them were tiny. Changes like this help scientists to trace the evolution of dinosaurs.

Although *Eoraptor* was not very big, it was very active and fierce. It hunted small creatures of the time, such as reptiles and insects.

NAYSAURUS

Dinosaurs quickly evolved into two groups: the meat-eaters and the plant-eaters. *Unaysaurus* was one of the earliest of the plant-eating groups. Like other dinosaurs of the time, *Unaysaurus* was smaller than many other animals around. Its later descendants were very much bigger – they were the massive long-necked sauropods such as *Brachiosaurus*.

Unaysaurus had teeth that were roughly serrated, like vegetable graters. It ate plants that grew on the ground and probably also stood on its hind legs, to reach leaves high up in trees.

Part of the *Unaysaurus* skeleton found in Brazil in 2004. From this, scientists can see that the hind legs of *Unaysaurus* were much longer and heavier than its front legs. This suggests that it was able to spend a lot of time on its hind legs.

ANIMAL FACTFILE

NAME: *Unaysaurus* (Black Water lizard, named after the area where it was found)

PRONOUNCED: you-na-sawr-us

GROUP: Prosauropod dinosaur

WHERE IT LIVED: Brazil

WHEN IT LIVED: Late Triassic Period (225 to 200 million years ago)

LENGTH: 2.4 metres

SPECIAL FEATURES: The earliest known of the long-necked plant-eaters

FOOD: Leaves and ferns

MAIN ENEMY: Big land-living crocodiles and early dinosaurs

DID YOU KNOW?: *Unaysaurus* was closely related to other dinosaurs found in North America, Germany and China. This shows the same kinds of animals lived all over the world at that time.

ANTETONITRUS

અનટેટોનાર્ટિસ

Antetonitrus was one of the first of the sauropods, a group of really big, long-necked plant-eaters. The sauropods evolved from the more primitive prosauropods in the late Triassic Period. *Antetonitrus* looked like the bigger members of the prosauropods. We can tell it was not the same by the different arrangement of bones in its feet.

Some of the trees of the late Triassic Period had tough sword-like leaves. This was to defend themselves against the new plant-eaters like *Antetonitrus*.

Later dinosaurs like *Camarasaurus* (pictured) looked very similar to *Antetonitrus*. *Camarasaurus* had a claw on the inner front toe to defend against predators. Perhaps *Antetonitrus* also had this adaptation.

COELOPHYSIS

The early meat-eating dinosaurs may have been small, but some of them made up for this in cunning. *Coelophysis* was one of the earliest of the meat-eaters. There is evidence that it hunted in packs. Pack-hunting animals can successfully hunt beasts much larger than themselves.

Coelophysis was probably a scavenger as well as a hunter, and ate almost anything it could find. Many types of fish and reptiles have been found in its stomach.

Two forms of *Coelophysis* fossil have been found. One form is thinner, and more delicate, than the other. It is thought they are male and female dinosaurs.

ANIMAL FACTFILE

NAME: *Coelophysis* (hollow form)

PRONOUNCED: see-low-fye-sis

GROUP: Theropod dinosaur

WHERE IT LIVED: Arizona and New Mexico

WHEN IT LIVED: Late Triassic Period (225 to 220 million years ago)

LENGTH: 3 metres — but most was neck and tail, and its body was about the same size as a fox

SPECIAL FEATURES: Lived and hunted in packs

FOOD: Other reptiles

MAIN ENEMY: Big land-living crocodiles

DID YOU KNOW?: A fossil skull of *Coelophysis* was taken on the space shuttle *Endeavour* in 1998. It was the first dinosaur in space!

LILIENSTERNUS

લીલીઅૈના ૨૨નસ

By the end of the Triassic Period, some of the dinosaurs were quite large. *Liliensternus* was one of the first big hunters. It was big enough to hunt and eat the earliest of the long-necked plant-eaters.

In 1802, footprints were found in some Triassic rocks in Connecticut, USA. They were thought to have been made by giant birds. However, after the discovery of fossils, such as this *Liliensternus*, it was realised that they were the footprints of meat-eating dinosaurs.

ANIMAL
FACTFILE

NAME: *Liliensternus* (from Hugo Ruele von Lilienstern – an early palaeontologist who originally discovered the fossils)

PRONOUNCED: Lil-ee-en-ster-nus

GROUP: Theropod dinosaur

WHERE IT LIVED: Germany, France

WHEN IT LIVED: Late Triassic Period (225 to 213 million years ago)

LENGTH: 6 metres

SPECIAL FEATURES: Large meat-eater with two crests on the head

FOOD: Other dinosaurs

MAIN ENEMY: None

DID YOU KNOW?: *Liliensternus* may have preyed on larger dinosaurs that were stuck in quicksand.

Two *Liliensternus* dinosaurs attack a prosauropod. This picture shows the crests on *Liliensternus's* head. It seems to have had two crests that ran from the nostrils to behind the eyes. They would have been used by the dinosaurs for signalling to each other.

CYNOGNATHUS

સાઈનાખ્યસ

One group of reptiles became very similar to mammals in Triassic times. They were probably warm-blooded, like mammals, and had a similar body shape. They might have even had fur. Eventually this group evolved into the mammals themselves, in the Triassic Period. *Cynognathus* was one of the most mammal-like of these reptiles.

Scientists think *Cynognathus* was covered in fur because the bones of its snout show tiny pits where whiskers would have been. Only furry animals have whiskers.

The skull of the *Cynognathus* is very similar to the skull of a mammal. Only the shape of the jaw shows that it was actually a reptile.

ANIMAL
FACTFILE

NAME: *Cynognathus* (dog jaw)

PRONOUNCED: sy-nog-nay-thus

GROUP: Therapsid group of mammal-like reptiles

WHERE IT LIVED: South Africa

WHEN IT LIVED: Middle Triassic Period (245 to 230 million years ago)

LENGTH: 1.5 metres

SPECIAL FEATURES: Teeth like a dog, with nipping incisors at the front, stabbing canines at the side, and meat-shearing molars at the back

FOOD: Other animals

MAIN ENEMY: The big land-living crocodiles

DID YOU KNOW?: The jawbone of *Cynognathus*, or something closely related, has been found in Antarctica. This shows that Africa and Antarctica were jointed together in Triassic times.

ANIMAL FAMILIES GLOSSARY

Aetosaur — a group of plant-eating reptiles, very closely related to the crocodiles. They were covered in armour and lived on land in the Triassic Period.

Ichthyosaur — the group of sea-going reptiles that were so well-adapted to living in the sea that they looked like dolphins or sharks, with fins on the tail and back and paddles for limbs. They were common in the Triassic and the Jurassic periods but died out in the Cretaceous.

Nothosaur — a sea reptile that had long jaws for catching fish, and webbed feet for swimming through water. Several kinds of nothosaur lived in the shallow waters around Europe and Asia in the Triassic Period.

Placodont — a group of swimming reptiles that fed on shellfish. Many had shells like turtles, although they were not related.

Prosauropod — an early dinosaur group that were plant-eaters and had long necks for reaching into trees. They were the biggest animals of the Triassic and early Jurassic, but not as big as their descendants — the sauropods.

Pterosaur — the flying reptiles of the age of dinosaurs. They had broad leathery wings supported on a long fourth finger, and were covered in hair to keep them warm.

Rauisuchian — a group of land-living meat-eaters of the Triassic Period, closely related to the crocodiles. They were the fiercest animals of the time.

Sauropod — the plant-eating dinosaur group that had the huge bodies, the long necks and the long tails. They were the biggest land-living animals that ever lived, and reached their peak in late Jurassic times.

Therapsid — the most mammal-like group of the mammal-like reptiles. They were covered in fur and had teeth like the teeth of a mammal. Some were so mammal-like that you would think they were dogs.

Theropod — the meat-eating dinosaur group. They all had the same shape — long jaws with sharp teeth, long strong hind legs, smaller front legs with clawed hands, and a small body balanced by a long tail.

LOSSARY

Adapted — changing to survive in a particular habitat or weather conditions.

Canines — strong, pointed teeth.

Carnivorous — an animal that eats meat.

Cunning — clever at getting what they want.

Dinosaur — large group of meat-eating or plant-eating reptiles that no longer exist.

Evolution — changes or developments that happen to all forms of life over millions of years, as a result of changes in the environment.

Evolve — to change or develop.

Fossils — the remains of a prehistoric plant or animal that has been buried for a long time and become hardened in rock.

Incisors — sharp-edged front teeth in the upper and lower jaws.

Lagoons — shallow ponds joined to seas or lakes.

Molars — special teeth used for grinding food.

Oases — green areas in a desert, where there is water and where plants grow.

Predators — animals that hunt and kill other animals for food.

Primitive — a very early stage in the development of a species.

Prosauropod — late Triassic Period ancestors of long-necked, plant-eating dinosaurs.

Reefs — ridges of rock, sand or coral near the surface of the sea

Reptiles — cold-blooded, crawling or creeping animals with a backbone.

Reptilian — animals that look like a reptile.

Serrated — having a jagged edge like a saw.

Snout — an animal's nose.

Species — a group of animals which all look like each other.

Streamlined — an animal with a smooth, bullet-shaped body so that it can move through air or water easily and quickly.

Trilobites — early type of sea animals that no longer exist.

Warm-blooded — animals, such as small mammals, which always have the same body temperature.

INDEX

PICTURE CREDITS

Main illustrations: 18-19 Lisa Alderson; 6-7, 8-9, 10-11 Simon Mendez;
22-23, 24-25, 26-27, 28-29 Luis Rey; 12-13, 14-15, 16-17, 20-21 Chris Tomlin

4TL, 4TR, 5 (Cenozoic Era), 6, 9, 11, 13, 14, 18, 21, 25, 26, 29 Ticktock Media archive; 5 (Mesozoic Era top,
Palaeozoic Era top) Simon Mendez; 5 (Mesozoic Era centre, Palaeozoic Era bottom) Luis Rey; 5 (Mesozoic Era bottom)
Lisa Alderson; 17 Chris Tomlin; 23 Phil Degginger/Carnegie Museum/Alamy

Every effort has been made to trace the copyright holders and we apologise in advance for any unintentional omissions.
We would be pleased to insert the appropriate acknowledgement in any subsequent edition of this publication.

CONTENTS

A double-edged longsword was often used by a knight to bring down his enemy.

STEEL AND STONE

Towering castles of stone still stand in Europe and western Asia, many of them in ruins. These massive strongholds have guarded mountain passes, rivers, seashores and towns since the Middle Ages. They remind us of the many centuries of hardship, war and conquest, when armoured knights rode out to do battle with the enemy.

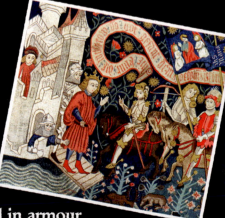

The girl in armour

Medieval tapestries and paintings reveal all sorts of details about armour and castles. This tapestry shows St Joan of Arc, a simple French peasant girl who was inspired by heavenly voices. She raised forces against the English invaders of her homeland. In 1429, she rode into battle dressed in full armour, like a knight.

> About 10,000 castles have been recorded in Spanish history. Remains of over 2,000 of them survive today.

Loarre Castle, in Aragon, an old kingdom in Spain, was built between about 1020 and the 1200s.

"Thou were the sternest knight to thy mortal foe [enemy] that ever [took up a] spear."

Sir Thomas Malory
Le Morte d'Arthur (The Death of Arthur), 1485

www.bbc.co.uk/history/british/middle_ages

Age of knights

Many people played their part in the medieval world. Peasants toiled on the land. Merchants traded in wool or wine. Women spun yarn and wove cloth. Priests led worship in the great cathedrals. The knights' job was to fight on horseback. Knights became powerful and famous, as loyal friends or as fierce enemies, as champions of the king – or as traitors...

FIRST KNIGHTS

In ancient times, fighters on horseback (the cavalry) were often lightly armed, allowing them to move quickly. But heavily armoured warriors were also used to smash through enemy lines, and during the Middle Ages, this type of cavalry became more and more important in warfare. Armed with swords and protected by helmets, these horsemen were the first knights.

KNIGHT – a warrior who served a lord during the Middle Ages in Europe and who often fought on horseback

Charging into battle
Heavy cavalry was used by the Persians more than 1,400 years ago, and also by their enemies, the Greeks of the Byzantine empire.

Swiss sword, c.1100

Brave and bold
A Persian silver bowl from about the 400s CE depicts a king as a mounted warrior, killing a lion. In later medieval Europe, too, kings liked to be shown as brave knights on horseback.

lion slayed by the king

Mighty swords
The great age of the European knights lasted from the 1000s to the 1400s. Knights would fight from the saddle, or on foot if they had been knocked to the ground. They used swords, axes and long spears called lances. Some knights also carried maces – clubs with spiky metal heads.

Italian sword, c.1400

⊜ A FIRM FOOTING

The stirrup was invented in Asia. By the 700s CE, it was being used throughout Europe. It held a horseman steady in the saddle, making it easier for him to swing a sword in battle. This single invention changed warfare forever.

This bronze stirrup was made in Asia more than 1,300 years ago.

> In England, a knight was given the respectful title 'Sir'.

Mask of metal

In about 600CE, most fighting men wore only simple helmets, but this Anglo-Saxon helmet was fit for a king. Decorated with panels that show battle scenes, it has eyebrows, a nose and a moustache, all made of gold covered with bronze. A crest wrapping over the top of the helmet is completed by two dragon heads with red gemstones for eyes.

The helmet's main framework was crafted from iron and its lining made of leather.

ceremonial axehead from Germany, 600s CE

iron inlaid with silver

Elite weapons

This rare, decorated axe, from the 600s CE, is Frankish (belonging to a tribe originating from modern-day Germany). During the age of the knights, weapons were important not just as fighting tools but as symbols of power and status.

replica of a ceremonial helmet from England in the early 600s CE

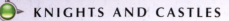

FIRST CASTLES

Earth, wood and stone have been used to build defences throughout human history. The great castle builders of the Middle Ages were the Normans. They were descended from the Vikings, who settled in northern France in 911 CE. During the following centuries, the Normans invaded parts of the British Isles, Italy and the Middle East. They built castles to defend their own lands and to control the lands that they conquered.

Castle keeps

Once the Normans decided to stay in the lands that they had invaded, they replaced their timber motte-and-bailey forts with stone towers called keeps or donjons. These castles were forts for local lords. Orford Castle (above) in Suffolk, England, was built between 1165 and 1173.

Motte-and-bailey settlements were protected from attack by walls, fences, ditches and forts. These castles could be built in as little as eight days.

bailey (enclosed area)

> Within 100 years of the Norman Conquest, which began in 1066, there were about 600 motte-and-bailey castles in England and Wales.

"Bishop Odo and Earl William... built castles far and wide throughout the land, oppressing the unhappy people."

An Anglo-Saxon describes the Normans, 1067

Soldiers force local people to do much of the building work.

Motte and bailey

When the Normans first invaded enemy territory, they often built temporary castles made of timber. These were defended by ditches and fences. A tower was raised on top of a motte, a high mound of soil and rocks. Below this was an enclosed area called a bailey. The castle site was guarded by soldiers during construction.

motte (raised earth mound)

A moat surrounds the castle.

MAIL – chain-mail, armour made from inter-linking iron rings

mail hood, or coif

helmet with a nasal, or nose bar

THE MEN OF MAIL

The Normans, once settled in northern France, sent their armies storming across Europe in the 1000s and 1100s. They invaded southern Italy and England. Norman knights swore loyalty to their lord and their services were rewarded with gifts of land and honours.

Norman shields were kite-shaped and made of wood and leather.

Chain-mail was strong but flexible.

The Bayeux Tapestry

This 70m-long strip of needlework tells the story of the Norman Conquest, when England fell under the control of its invaders. The Normans won their most famous victory when they defeated the Anglo-Saxons near Hastings, England, in 1066. Here, chain-mail shirts and weapons are supplied to the Norman knights.

Norman chain-mail

The Norman knights of the 1000s and 1100s wore armour of mail. To make this, thick iron wire was shaped into rings around a wooden or metal rod. Each ring was cut off, linked with four others and then closed by a rivet, or fastener. A mail coat called a hauberk was worn over a padded tunic and leggings called chausses.

> About 6,000 soldiers – and more than 600 horses – may have died at the Battle of Hastings in 1066.

The great helm

In the year 1250, European knights were still wearing mail armour. Over the hauberk, they now wore a cloth tunic called a surcoat. Instead of the simple helmet with a nasal (nose bar), some knights now wore the great helm, which looked like a bucket with eye slits.

"You could see the blood flowing through the mail, from a wound made by the keen sword that Dietrich wielded."

The Song of the Nibelungs, c.1200

The great helm covered the whole head. It was padded on the inside.

The gauntlet had a wide cuff to protect the hand.

The hauberk weighed about 10kg.

Dismounted by blows from a lance, two knights turn on their attackers for hand-to-hand combat.

● WEAPONS OF WAR

swords, c.1300s

mace, c.1100s

battle axe, c.1000s

In the 1000s, the sword was chiefly used for slashing and cutting, but by the late 1200s, swords were being designed to pierce through chain-mail for deadly thrusts to the body. A blow from a mace (a type of club with a spiked metal head) or from a battle axe could also break through mail and cause a severe injury. Knights had to use shields as their main defence against weapons.

THE CRUSADES

"...there was at least an acre of land behind the Templars, which was so covered with arrows fired by the Saracens that none of the ground could be seen."

John of Johnville
February 11, 1250

In 1095, Pope Urban II called upon Christian knights from western Europe to fight the Muslims, or Saracens, living in the Holy Land – the region now occupied by Syria, Lebanon, Israel, Palestine and Egypt. A series of savage conflicts followed. These are known as the Crusades, or 'wars of the cross'.

A Saracen fights with a sword and round shield. Saracens also used bows and arrows.

CRUSADES – military expeditions by medieval Christians, including the attempt to capture the Holy Land from the Muslims

CRUSADER STEEL

sword, early 1300s

falchion, 1200s

lance, c.1100s

flail, 1500s

helmet, c.1200s

Weapons included straight swords and curved falchions, which had a single cutting edge. Flails were sticks with spiked balls. Some helmets of the 1200s were flat-topped while others had rounded caps.

> Crusades were also fought against Muslims in Spain and against non-Christians in eastern Europe.

Fierce battles

As armoured knights battled in the heat and dust, cities were conquered and civilians were massacred. If captured, a knight was sometimes held prisoner until a ransom was paid for his release. In 1204, the Crusaders even attacked fellow Christians, sacking the city of Constantinople (modern Istanbul). They left the Holy Land in 1291.

Like other Crusaders, this knight of the Templar order wears a cross to symbolize his Christian faith.

Krak des Chevaliers in Syria was one of the strongest castles built by the Saracens.

www.historyforkids.org/learn/medieval/history/highmiddle/bernard.htm

FIGHTING ORDERS

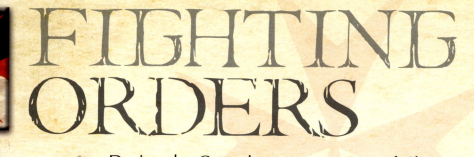

During the Crusades, some groups of Christian knights took religious vows, forming special organisations or orders. In 1096, the Templars were founded to protect pilgrims travelling to Jerusalem. The Hospitallers, or Knights of St John, dated from 1113. They vowed to protect the sick and the poor. Both orders won fame on the battlefield.

14th-century engraving of a knight Templar

Rise to power
The knights were formidable fighters who guarded the great castles built by the Crusaders across the Holy Land. But the orders were not just fighting forces – from simple beginnings, the Hospitallers and Templars became wealthy organisations with great political power in Europe.

ORDER – a religious organisation of Christian knights or a special group of knights honoured by a monarch

Hospitallers made their vows on this silver cross inlaid with gemstones.

Battling monks
The orders of knights had strict rules and expected their members to live like monks.

knight Hospitaller, 1530s

Walls of Malta
After the Christians were forced out of the Holy Land, the Hospitallers moved their headquarters to various Mediterranean islands – Cyprus from 1291, Rhodes from 1309 and Malta (left) from 1530.

🔴 SIGNS OF THE CROSS

The knights of the Templar and Hospitaller orders both had their own emblems. The Templars had a red cross on white, whereas the Hospitallers had a white cross on black. The Teutonic Knights from Germany were another Christian order and so their emblem was also based on the cross. They too had fought in the Holy Land, but later they operated in eastern and central Europe and in areas around the Baltic Sea.

Knights Templar

Knights Hospitaller

Teutonic Knights

> The Templars took their name from the Temple of Solomon in Jerusalem, a city holy to Jews, Christians and Muslims.

"It is not easy for anyone to gain an idea of the power and wealth of the Templars... for they... have built castles everywhere..."

Theoderich
Description of the Holy Places, c.1172

Marienburg, or Malbork, Castle in Poland was built by the Teutonic Knights in 1274.

A Teutonic knight fights a Polish knight during the Battle of Grunwald, 1410.

www.templarhistory.com

The Teutonic Knights

These knights became the most powerful force in eastern Europe. However, on one day in 1410, the strength of the Teutonic order was broken forever. They were defeated by a Lithuanian and Polish army during a massive battle at Grunwald in Poland.

Doom of the Templars

Everyone was jealous of the Templars' riches and power, especially King Philip IV of France. In 1307, he accused the order of the most terrible crimes. Templars were imprisoned and tortured and all their wealth was seized.

This sketch shows an effigy, or statue, on the tomb of a Templar in the Temple Church in London.

BUILDING IN STONE

"...we have needed... 400 masons, both cutters and layers, together with 2,000 less-skilled workmen, 100 carts, 60 wagons and 30 boats bringing stone..."

Master James of St George, architect of Beaumaris Castle, Wales, *c.1295*

Stone castles soon replaced the early wooden structures, with round towers beginning to replace square ones. The keep, or stronghold, was now surrounded by massive inner and outer walls and sometimes by a moat full of water, crossed by a drawbridge. By the 1290s, castle keeps were surrounded by a series of ring defences. These 'concentric' castles (see plans for Caerphilly and Coca castles overleaf) enabled archers on the high inner walls to fire over the heads of archers on the lower outer walls.

CONCENTRIC CASTLE – a type of castle with rings of defensive walls surrounding a central point

⬤ TOOLS OF THE TRADE

With only basic iron tools and muscle power, the skilled medieval craftsmen worked wonders. Carpenters sawed and hammered, while masons chiselled the stone and checked that the walls were strong and straight.

carpenter's axe

handsaw

awl

mason's axe

mallet

chisel

frame-saw

Wooden scaffolding helps the stonemasons to build the gatehouse.

A soldier, one of a force guarding the workers, practises archery.

The architect worries about building costs.

Quarried stone is delivered by river barges and then ox-carts.

This crane is powered by a worker walking inside a treadwheel.

> The walls of the great tower at Flint Castle in Wales were 7m thick.

Roof tiles were made from slate (shown here) or ceramic (baked clay).

The workforce

Often thousands of workers were drafted in to the building site. Timber was cut in the forest, and labourers dug ditches and raised wooden scaffolding as the new castle began to rise. To make a single, massive defensive wall, rubble and mortar (a mixture of sand, lime and water) were poured between twin walls of stone.

The battlements will have low 'embrasures' and high 'merlons', so that archers can fire or take cover.

Mortar, made from sand, lime and water, binds the stone.

THE BIG CASTLES

The castles of Europe and western Asia changed greatly as the years passed. Some fell into ruin, while others were altered to deal with new threats or social changes. Building styles varied from time to time and place to place, and many were rebuilt or enlarged in a new style. Some of these big castles still inspire awe today.

Castillo de Coca, Spain

This castle was built for a powerful archbishop during the reign of King Henry IV of Castile. Its builders were Moors – Muslims from Spain and northern Africa. The decorative brick construction of its powerful walls was a traditional style from Muslim lands.

This concentric castle was built at the end of the 15th century.

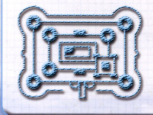

Hrad Rabí, Czech Republic

This massive castle stands in the old kingdom of Bohemia and dates back to the 1200s. It may have been built to protect local trading routes or goldmining operations. The castle was captured in the 1420s, and much of it was rebuilt in later years.

One-eyed General Zizka successfully besieged Rabí in 1421, despite losing the use of his one good eye.

Château Gaillard, France

Towering above the River Seine, this amazing castle was built for King Richard I of England, Duke of Normandy. It took just one year to build, from 1197 to 1198. After a long siege, the castle fell to the French in 1204.

More than 6,000 labourers helped to build the castle.

> Some stone castles were originally painted white. Others relied on decorative carvings to look impressive.

The elaborate brickwork of the castle's towers are typical of Moorish architecture.

Marksburg, Germany

The lords of this magnificent German castle grew rich by charging shipping tolls on the River Rhine. Between 1283 and 1479, the stronghold was rebuilt by the powerful counts of Katzenelnbogen.

The first written records about the castle date back to 1231.

The Spanish Castillo de Coca rises out of a deep, 560m-long moat.

Caerphilly Castle, Wales, UK

The English baron Gilbert de Clare seized this part of Wales in 1266. To defend it from recapture by the Welsh, he built a great concentric castle with twin walls and surrounded it with a broad, water-filled moat. Today, much of the castle remains in its original condition.

Building began in 1268, but in 1270, the castle was attacked and damaged before it was finished. It was rebuilt in 1271.

Alcázar de Segovia, Spain

A stronghold was built here in Roman times and a castle (*alcázar*) also dated from the period of Muslim rule. From the 1100s to the 1500s, the castle was repeatedly rebuilt by the Christian kings of Castile.

The castle is shaped like the bow (front) of a ship, with its tallest tower as the mast.

CHÂTELAINE – a lady who is in charge of running a castle

CASTLE LIFE

A castle was not just a fortress, it was a home for many people. It might have belonged to a powerful lord or been held by him on behalf of the king. A large castle was occupied by the lord's family as well as his steward (the castle manager), knights, soldiers, tax collectors, servants, cooks and huntsmen.

Changing times

In the early Middle Ages, castles, which were built for defence and conquest, offered very little privacy or comfort. By the 1400s, many lords and ladies wanted more luxurious homes, so some castles were slowly converted into grand palaces.

Châtelaine

While the lord is away at war, his affairs are run by his wife, the lady of the castle, or châtelaine. She holds all the keys and runs the household from day to day. Here, she stands in the great hall, giving orders.

Priest

The castle has its own chapel, a tall chamber whose window glows with colourful stained glass. It is decorated with stories from the Bible. In front of the altar, the priest leads the prayers for the castle household, and knights pray here before battle.

Blacksmith

In a corner of the courtyard, a smith hammers away at his anvil, which he is using to shape and repair iron tools, weapons, chains, buckets, wheel rims, horseshoes and bars for the portcullis (metal gate).

prison

store-room

work shop
3

chapel
2

1

 Toilets (garderobes) had stone seats over open shafts that dropped down to a sewage pit – or the moat.

KEY

🟥 lower levels

🟦 ground floor

🟩 first floor

great hall

kitchen **4**

courtyard

Round towers required spiral staircases made of stone. These were easy to defend from an attack, but were hard work for servants carrying jugs of wine or pails of water.

solar **5**

Walls could be up to 5m thick in places.

6 lord's bedroom

toilet (garderobe)

Servants

Servants attend to the lord and lady, pick herbs from the garden, prepare food, wash clothes, fetch water from the well and firewood from the yard. They also make beds, light lanterns, snuff out candles, sweep the floors and clean out the stables.

The eldest son

The lord's eldest son plays a board game in the solar, the private living room of the family. The solar is a large room on the first floor. It is warm and sunny in the summer but cold in the winter, when it needs to be heated by a large fireplace.

Lord of the castle

The lord of the castle prepares for bed. The castle rooms have little furniture compared with a modern house. Linen, clothes and valuable goods are kept in big chests on the floor. The four-poster bed has curtains to keep out cold draughts.

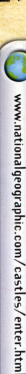

GREAT HALL

The centre of activity in many castles was the great hall. This was a lofty room with tall windows and a high, timbered roof. Its walls were hung with tapestries, and the floor strewn with sweet-smelling rushes. Logs would blaze in a huge fireplace, but it could be cold and draughty in winter.

great hall of Warwick Castle, England

> "Take hocks of venison and partly boil them in salted water... make pastry and place the venison on it. Season all over with ground pepper, ginger and salt. Place in oven..."
>
> **Recipe for venison (deer) pie,** *1400s*

Youngsters were taught how to serve food as part of their training for knighthood.

Fanfare for a feast

By the 1400s, fine table manners were an important part of courtly life. Here, trumpets sound as French ladies are served dainty dishes. The music may continue in the hall after supper, when the trumpeters might be joined by musicians playing harps, flutes and drums.

Heart of the castle

Today, the great hall of this English castle displays suits of armour and old weapons. In the Middle Ages, the halls were not just places to entertain with feasts and music. They also served as places for meetings between a lord and his knights to discuss future battles. The great hall was also used to put traitors on trial.

🔴 FROM THE KITCHEN

A noble banquet might include enormous pies, fine white rolls, roasted swan or wild boar. Meat was stewed in cauldrons or roasted on spits. Ordinary people ate simple food, such as crusts of coarse bread, cheese, broth or porridge.

roast pheasants and sauce

Great banquets

A high table for noble or royal guests stood at one end of the great hall, covered with fine linen. It was laid with silver cups, plates, spoons and knives. (Forks were not used until the end of the Middle Ages, and diners often used their hands to eat.) In the lower part of the hall, people sat on benches at simple board tables. They ate off wooden plates or just thick slabs of bread called trenchers.

John of Gaunt (1340–1399), son of King Edward III of England, dines with the King of Portugal and four bishops.

This 'round table', hanging in the great hall of Winchester Castle, England, was painted in the 1500s with the names of the mythical knights of King Arthur.

www.castlewales.com/life.html

CASTLE TOWNS

Many medieval castles were built on the site of ancient strongholds, where towns had already developed over the ages. In recently conquered lands, castles were built on new sites and new towns were built alongside them. The towns were surrounded by high walls and fortified gatehouses that joined up with the castle defences. The lord of the castle profited from the townspeople's trade and taxes.

TOWN CHARTERS

New towns were authorized by the king in a document called a charter, which was sealed with wax. This seal, from about 1316, is from Conwy, a walled castle town in northern Wales.

butcher chopping venison (deer meat)

edible snails for sale

> By the 1400s, some merchants and bankers were becoming richer than the lords in their castles.

www.britainexpress.com/History/Townlife.htm

A walled city

The city of Carcassonne in southwestern France has been fortified since the days of the Celts and the Romans. Its massive medieval defences include double walls and 53 towers. For centuries, Carcassonne was the scene of religious turmoil and warfare.

God's fortress

Medieval Europe was famous for its great cathedrals and abbeys as well as its castles. The settlements around these religious buildings had to be defended from attack with great walls. The island monastery and church of Mont St Michel is in Normandy, France. The English tried to capture it from 1423 to 1424.

Mont St Michel is defended by the ocean as well as its walls – it could be reached on foot only at low tide.

fishmonger and barrel

baker's cart

Market day

Castles controlled the economic life of the lands they ruled. Their towns had busy streets with shops and market stalls selling food, woollen cloth or leather goods. There were blacksmiths, coopers (barrel-makers) and wheelwrights, who made and repaired wheels. And there were inns selling ale and wine, where travellers could rest and stable their horses.

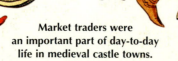

Market traders were an important part of day-to-day life in medieval castle towns.

FEUDAL SYSTEM – *a society based upon grants of land, duties and responsibilities*

CASTLE LANDS

The castle and surrounding lands were granted to the lord by the king in return for an oath of loyalty. The knights swore allegiance to the lord, who promised to protect them and their lands in return. The peasants who worked in the fields had few rights under this 'feudal system'. Some were not even allowed to move away or seek other work.

Fruits of labour

As far as the eye could see, the lands around the castle were governed – and taxed – by the lord of the castle. The lord also owned the watermills or windmills, which ground the wheat or barley. Farmers and labourers had to provide both the castle and the church with food produce. Here, the farm workers are harvesting crops and shearing sheep.

May Day dances

fashionable court dress of the 15th century

Knights and ladies celebrated May Day with dancing (left), games and picnics. They rode out into the countryside, sometimes carrying sprigs of greenery to welcome in the season of sunshine and new growth.

> Castle lands kept by the lord for his own use were known as the demesne.

http://library.thinkquest.org/10949/fief/medfeudal.html

The ploughman

Strong oxen were used for hauling farm wagons and ploughs. Crops were grown on strips of land with no hedges in between. Cattle and sheep grazed on common land.

Four seasons

In the autumn, just after the ploughing, the land was harrowed (below left) to smooth the soil. Then seed was scattered by hand (below right). The labourers worked hard during all seasons because if the harvest failed, famine would follow.

The hawkers

Groups of nobles took birds of prey from the castle's mews (falconry sheds) to go hunting. The hawks and falcons were trained to catch small animals such as pheasants, rabbits and ducks. Hunting with hounds was also popular.

Hawking, or falconry, was a formal activity for which nobles would dress in their finest clothes.

SIEGE

SIEGE – the attack of a castle or city by surrounding it, often cutting it off from supplies of food and water

To win control of a region, an army first had to capture local castles and cities. The soldiers surrounded the walls and cut off all supplies and support. This was called a siege. The aim was to force the surrender of the castle, preferably before it was too damaged. If this failed, the attackers would try to climb over the walls, smash them down, or dig under them until they collapsed.

Various types of catapult were used to hurl missiles at the walls or over the battlements. Cannons did not come into use until the 1340s.

trebuchet (a catapult that used a counterweight)

mangonel (a catapult that hurled rocks from a cup at the end of its arm)

pavise (protective shield)

All-out assault

The attackers have stripped the countryside bare of food. Now their spies tell them that an army is on the way to relieve the castle. They have no time to lose. They launch a desperate final attack with huge catapults, battering rams and siege towers. Arrows rain down on the castle.

> The French claimed to have broken a siege at Château Gaillard in 1204 by crawling in through the toilet shafts.

Siege towers were nicknamed belfries, because they looked like the bell tower of a church.

scaling ladder

battering ram with protective covering

DEFENCE

Castles were designed for defence. With secure supplies of food and fresh water, even small garrisons could withstand a siege for many months. They were protected by massive walls and towers, by moats and battlements. Dangers were posed by weak points in the defences, by traitors letting in the enemy, by starvation or disease.

Wooden 'hourds' stick out beyond the walls, enabling defenders to shoot arrows or drop rocks from them.

GATEHOUSE DEFENCE

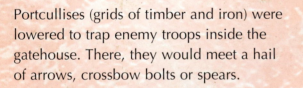

Portcullises (grids of timber and iron) were lowered to trap enemy troops inside the gatehouse. There, they would meet a hail of arrows, crossbow bolts or spears.

Rocks, boiling water or even heated sand could be dropped onto the troops below, through openings in the ceiling known as meurtriers, or murder holes.

To the last man

Enemy soldiers are already swarming over a section of wall. A body of attacking knights has broken through the gatehouse and is rushing the defending troops, who are offering stiff resistance. The defenders have been erecting wooden fighting platforms, or hourds, around the towers, but these have been set on fire and badly damaged by rocks catapulted by the enemy. Defenders, in their desperation, may now risk counter-attacking the enemy camp.

> At the siege of Caffa (1346), Mongol troops catapulted dead bodies over their walls to spread disease among the enemy.

A defender prepares to pour boiling liquid onto the attackers.

gatehouse

Supplies of food and equipment are destroyed by fire.

Soldiers struggle to see in the smoke.

THE MEN OF PLATE

Mail could be pierced by a well-aimed arrow or a spear, so in the years after 1220, knights began to use a new type of armour. They protected parts of their bodies with plates of solid steel. In the years that followed, more and more plates were added. By the 1400s, the whole body was encased in metal.

Metal-workers

Here, an armourer hammers away in his workshop. Each city identified the armour that it made with its own unique mark. Famous centres included Milan in Italy, and Augsburg and Nuremberg in Germany. The most expensive plate armour was specially made to fit the wearer.

HELMETS

The sallet was a helmet used from the 1430s until about 1500. It was often worn with a bevor, a collar protecting the chin and neck.

sallet

The basinet (or 'little basin') was used from the 1200s. From the 1390s to the 1450s, it often had a pointed visor (a hinged section protecting the eyes and face). The snout-like shape was designed to deflect blows to the face.

visor

holes for breathing

basinet

The steel plates of 15th-century armour were separate but joined by leather straps. This made it flexible, allowing free movement during battle.

shirt of mail

Knights in shining armour

By the 1400s, plate armour offered the best possible protection for a knight. The finest suits of armour, or harnesses, were custom-made for kings and princes, and they cost a fortune. However, even they could be pierced by a metal-tipped bolt fired from a powerful crossbow or battered by heavy blows from a sword.

www.metmuseum.org/toah/hd/rarm/hd_rarm.htm

A knight from about 1425 wears a mixture of mail and plate armour.

gauntlet

cuisse

This knight and horse from about 1475 are wearing only plate armour.

bevor

pauldron

poleyn

greave

"A horse! A horse! My kingdom for a horse!"

King Richard III's cry after his horse is killed in battle
Richard III, William Shakespeare, 1591

solleret

Gauntlet

The first knights protected their hands with long mail sleeves. From the 1300s, jointed plates were used to cover the hands, with metal cuffs over the wrists. This armour, called a gauntlet, was worn over a leather glove.

BATTLE

Knights thundered into battle on huge warhorses. They aimed to knock the enemy knights from their saddles with lances, and then attack them with swords and maces. Footsoldiers tried to dismount knights with long pikes. From the 1300s, the powerful longbow delivered murderous flights of arrows, to bring down horses and terrorize the enemy ranks.

WARHORSE – a type of horse, such as the powerful destrier, bred and trained for battle

Mud and blood

After the charge, there is confusion, terror and desperate hand-to-hand fighting. Victory was often decided by weather conditions or the choice of battlefield. The bloody Battle of Poitiers was one of the conflicts between the English and French during the Hundred Years' War. The war actually lasted from 1337 to 1453.

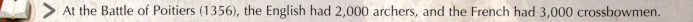
At the Battle of Poitiers (1356), the English had 2,000 archers, and the French had 3,000 crossbowmen.

CROSSBOWS AND BOLTS

Crossbows were small bows mounted on a shaft called a stock. They were extremely powerful and fired a short, heavy arrow known as a bolt. However, crossbows needed winding up and were slower to use than the longbow.

Steel crossbows were used from the 1300s.

Spikes called caltrops were laid on the battlefield to injure the enemy's horses. Pointed wooden stakes called palings (see below) were also used to deter cavalry.

caltrop with four spikes

Edward, the Black Prince, rallies the English troops.

vair

ermine

fess

pale

bend

bend sinister

HERALDRY

The feudal system of the 1000s and 1100s encouraged personal loyalties. Knights pledged allegiance to individuals or families rather than to a nation. Personal emblems, or charges, began to appear on shields, surcoats, horse trappings and pennants (see below). They were designed according to the strict rules of heraldry.

Herald

Heralds knew all about the designs on shields and the rules of warfare and tournaments. They discussed terms of fighting with the enemy and identified knights killed in battle.

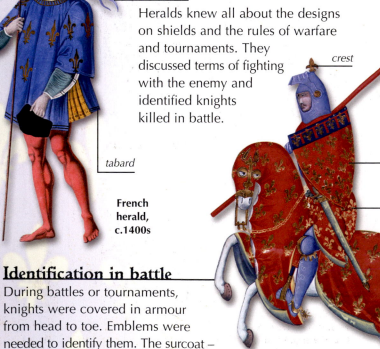

tabard

French herald, c.1400s

crest

pennant

shield

surcoat

trappings

Italian knight, early 1300s

Identification in battle

During battles or tournaments, knights were covered in armour from head to toe. Emblems were needed to identify them. The surcoat – and then just its emblems – became known as a coat-of-arms.

Patterns and rules

The rules of heraldry laid out in great detail the colours to be used, the basic ordinaries (patterns), and the emblems representing materials, weapons, flowers, birds or animals. Coats-of-arms are still used today by all sorts of organisations, and the same rules still apply.

● PARTS OF A SHIELD

in chief (top)

dexter (bearer's right)

sinister (bearer's left)

field (background)

charge (image)

in base (bottom)

This shield represented the Holy Roman emperors, who ruled large areas of Germany, central Europe and Italy. It shows the 'charge' (emblem or image) of an eagle, which is 'displayed' (with outstretched wings). The eagle is 'sable' (black) on a field of 'or' (gold) and is 'langued gules' (with a red tongue).

 > Mythical monsters were popular on shields. They included dragons and griffins.

chevron

pall

chief

cross

saltire

pile

The House of Plantagenet

A ruling family is known as a dynasty or house. This family came from Anjou in France and went on to rule Normandy, England, Jerusalem, Gascony and Guyenne (in France). The dynasty later became known as Plantagenet, because its founder, Geoffrey V of Anjou (1113–1151), was said to wear a sprig of broom flower (*plante genest*) in his hat.

King Richard I of England (1157–1199) was a grandson of Geoffrey of Anjou. He was a Crusader known as Coeur de Lion, or Lionheart. His shield bore three lions.

King Richard I, the Lionheart

Four generations later, Edward III (1312–1377) claimed the French throne, and combined (quartered) the English royal arms with the lilies (fleurs-de-lys) of France.

King Edward III

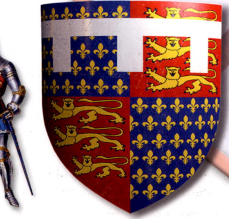

Edward III's eldest son was Edward, the Black Prince (1330–1376). His shield had a 'label argent' (silver bar) to show he was the king's son. He never became king himself.

Edward III's third son was John of Gaunt (1340–1399). Marrying into the royal family of Castile and León in Spain, he quartered the arms once again, to include a castle and a single lion.

Edward, the Black Prince

John of Gaunt

www.heraldry.ca/kids_en/heraldry_make_shield.htm

TOURNAMENT

Knights needed to practise their fighting skills. Free-for-all mock battles, or mêlées, were held along with bruising bouts of single combat, known as jousting. Soon splendid festivals called tournaments became popular, where knights could show off their bravery, their horsemanship and chivalry (noble behaviour).

For the ladies
A knight might dedicate his jousting contest to a lady of the court seated in the stands. He was identified by his coat-of-arms.

JOUSTING – a competition between two knights on horseback who are usually armed with lances

In 1179, about 3,000 knights took part in a single tournament held in northern France by King Louis VII.

At full tilt

In the 1400s, a type of jousting called tilting became fashionable. The knights, separated by a fence, thundered towards each other, aiming to dismount their opponent. Lances had blunt tips, but injuries could still be severe, so padded helmets and strengthened armour were worn.

A tournament is held at a castle in Germany in the 1400s.

www.middle-ages.org.uk/history-of-jousting.htm

🔴 FANTASY FIGHTING

This comic helmet was given as a present to King Henry VIII of England from the Emperor Maximilian I. It was designed for the pageants and entertainments that were often staged during tournaments.

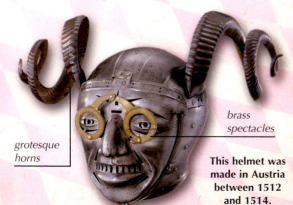

grotesque horns

brass spectacles

This helmet was made in Austria between 1512 and 1514.

CHIVALRY – the ideal virtues of the knight, such as courage, honour, respect, generosity and courtesy

THE CODE OF HONOUR

From the 1100s onwards, knights across Europe were expected to behave honourably and to follow Christian teachings. They were supposed to be courteous, gentle and noble, and to protect the weak from the strong. This code of honour was called chivalry. Wonderful poems were written about the ideals of knighthood – but the reality was often rather different.

The Black Prince

Edward the Black Prince (1330–1376) was named after the colour of some of his armour. The son of the English king, he was famous for his chivalry on the battlefield, treating enemy knights with respect and generosity. He was less chivalrous towards peasants, taxing them heavily and burning down their villages during war.

tomb of the Black Prince

Becoming a knight

Heinrich von Ulm is made a knight by Emperor Sigismund, in Germany in about 1415. A sword blade is tapped on each of the young man's shoulders, 'dubbing' him a knight. Such a ceremony would follow a vigil, a long night of praying in the chapel.

● PAGE TO SQUIRE

A French knight of the 1300s is armed by his squire.

At about seven years old, a boy was sent to a castle to serve as a page. He would learn good manners and fighting skills. When he was about 14, he could become a squire, assisting a knight on and off the battlefield. Once he had proved himself in battle, he too could become a knight.

> In the year 1308, there were probably about 1,250 knights in the whole of England.

www.middle-ages.org.uk/steps-to-knighthood.htm

In love with love

Knights were in love with the idea of love. Poets were always writing about chivalrous knights who honoured a pure, noble lady with little hope of winning her affection. This 'fine' or 'courtly' love had nothing do with real passion – nor with marriage, which was more about winning wealth or power.

Love – or Death!

This shield was made at the end of the 15th century. It was designed for a parade, not a real battle, and shows a young knight courting his lady. He swears that if she rejects his love, the figure of Death (far right) will carry him away.

French painting, 1475

A noble lady is seated in her castle.

A knight kneels before her, pledging his service.

A ring for the champion

The winner in a mock battle, or tournament, is awarded a ring by a young lady of the court. He wears a sword and spurs, both symbols of knighthood, and he is carrying a lance. As the Middle Ages drew to a close, tournaments became the last, splendid displays of chivalrous behaviour.

The keep of Mértola Castle, Portugal, was built in 1292.

Too expensive to maintain, roofs collapsed in the rain and wind, and walls fell into ruin.

PALACE – *a large, luxurious residence belonging to a king or a lord*

The knight, once loyal to his lord, was now expected to be loyal to his nation.

THE ROAD TO RUIN

By the 1500s, the age of knights and castles was coming to an end. There was still great interest in chivalry and tournaments, but the introduction of gunpowder had changed the nature of real warfare. Society had changed, too. Kings enjoyed showing off their grand palaces and capital cities. They wanted to keep their powerful nobles close to them in the royal court, rather than away in distant castles, where they could plot rebellions.

Many castles fell into ruin when local people stole the stones to build farms and homes.

Cannon power

Many of the last big attacks on surviving European castles occurred during the Thirty Years' War (1618–1648) and the English Civil War (1642–1646). Cannonballs could pound castle walls into rubble.

Cannons used gunpowder to fire round shots over long distances. Stone cannonballs were later replaced by iron ones.

A musketeer is a soldier armed with a musket, a long-barrelled gun that is fired from the shoulder.

www.castles-of-britain.com/castle49

THE AGE OF GUNPOWDER

In the 1500s and 1600s, smaller hand-held firearms also played their part in battle. Pistols were small and light, which helped troops to be mobile and fast. Suits of plate armour were also adapted to avoid weighing down the soldiers. Light cavalry wore less-bulky half-armour, which protected only the upper parts of the body and the thighs.

English breastplate and tassets (armour to protect the upper legs), c.1575

English matchlock musket, c.1640

German wheel-lock pistol, c.1580

German wheel-lock pistol, c.1640

Knights today

Modern knights gather at Windsor Castle, England. In some countries, medieval orders of knights have survived, and knighthood is awarded as an honour to leading citizens.

GLOSSARY

allegiance
Loyalty to a lord or a ruler.

Anglo-Saxon
One of the Germanic peoples who invaded England from the 5th century CE. The word 'knight' comes from *cniht* in the Anglo-Saxon language.

anvil
A heavy iron block on which hot metal is hammered into shape by a blacksmith.

battlements
The upper part of a fortified wall. Its high sections were called merlons and its low sections were called embrasures or crenels.

Byzantine empire
This was originally the eastern part of the Roman empire, ruled from the city of Constantinople (now Istanbul). Its armies developed the use of heavy cavalry in the early Middle Ages.

cavalry
Any soldiers who fought on horseback, including knights.

Celts
Various peoples living in central and western Europe in ancient times, including the Gauls, Britons, Gaels and Celt-Iberians. Celts were skilled iron-workers who used chain-mail at an early date.

chivalry
A code of honour that inspired knights in the later Middle Ages. It included such ideals as courage, courtesy and generosity towards enemies.

Christian
A follower of the Christian faith. The lands under Christian rule in the Middle Ages were known as Christendom.

concentric castle
A castle in which the central part is surrounded by rings of defensive walls and towers.

economic
Relating to work, trade or money.

embrasure
A low section of a castle's battlements through which an archer can fire arrows.

feudal system
A way of organizing society so that land is given out in return for services and pledges of loyalty.

fort
A defensive building designed as a military base rather than a private home.

griffin
An imaginary beast with the body of a lion and the wings of an eagle.

Holy Land
Those lands of western Asia held to be sacred by Jews, Christians and Muslims.

Jew
A follower of the faith of Judaism. The first Jewish, or Hebrew, people lived in western Asia.

keep
A castle's central tower, with thick walls.

lance
A type of long spear, designed to knock opponents to the ground. It was used by knights when charging on horseback.

medieval

Dating from or relating to the Middle Ages.

merlon

A high section of a castle's battlements that provides cover for an archer.

Middle Ages

The period between the classical age and the modern age. It is sometimes taken to start with the fall of the western Roman empire in 476CE and to last about 1,000 years.

monastery

A building in which monks live, work and worship.

Muslim

A follower of the Islamic faith. During the Middle Ages, Muslims lived in western Asia, northern Africa and Spain.

nobles

Families of the highest social class.

Persians

A people living in Persia (modern Iran) who were founders of several ancient and medieval empires.

pike

A long spear used by footsoldiers against cavalry in the 1400s.

portcullis

A heavy grid of timber and iron, designed to seal off a castle gatehouse when under attack.

quarried

Cut from a quarry of rocks. Quarried stone was transported to the site of a new castle, where it was carved, shaped and used to build walls.

Roman empire

The lands ruled by Rome in the period before the Middle Ages. They included much of western and southern Europe, western Asia and northern Africa.

Romans

A people living in Italy in ancient times who conquered a large empire.

siege

An attempt to force a castle or town to surrender or be captured by cutting off its supplies and communications and by attacking its defences.

steward

An official who managed the running of a castle and its affairs.

surcoat

A cloth tunic worn over clothing or armour.

tapestry

A hand-woven textile featuring patterns or pictures, used as wall hangings in many old castles.

tax

A charge of goods or money that must be paid to those governing the land.

traitor

Someone who breaks allegiance, betraying his or her loyalty.

trappings

Coverings of fabric placed over a knight's horse, also known as a caparison.

Vikings

Medieval warriors from Denmark, Sweden or Norway. The Normans were descendants of the Vikings who lived in northern France.

INDEX

INVESTIGATE

Find out how the experts know about knights and medieval life, and explore history by checking out books, websites, castles and museums.

15th-century manuscript

Written sources

Decorated manuscripts recount stories, poems or songs about knights and battles, while official documents give clues about medieval laws and accounts.

📖 *The Story of King Arthur* retold by Robin Lister (Kingfisher)

✦ The British Library, 96 Euston Road, London, UK, NW1 2DB

🌐 www.fitzmuseum.cam.ac.uk/pharos/images/swf/manuscript/manuscript_5a.html

tapestry depicting a grape harvest

Medieval art

Visit an art gallery to search for medieval tapestries or paintings, which can reveal the clothes people wore, the weapons they carried and how they entertained themselves.

📖 *Art of the Middle Ages* by Jennifer Olmstead (Heinemann)

✦ The National Gallery, Trafalgar Square, London, UK, WC2N 5DN

🌐 http://panograph.free.fr/BayeuxTapestry.html

Temple Church, London

Castles and churches

Some castles offer re-enactments of tournaments or battles, and some churches house the tombs of knights. Don't forget to look up – coats-of-arms are often displayed high on walls and ceilings.

📖 *The Best-Ever Book of Castles* by Philip Steele

✦ Temple Church, Temple, London, UK, EC4Y 7BB

🌐 www.castleuk.net/homepage.htm

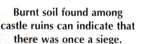

Burnt soil found among castle ruins can indicate that there was once a siege.

Archaeology

An excavation at a castle might find pottery, cannonballs, armour or even skeletons. Contact the Young Archaeologists' Club (weblink below left) to try to join a dig.

📖 *Kingfisher Knowledge: Archaeology* by Trevor Barnes (Kingfisher)

✦ Royal Armouries Museum, Armouries Drive, Leeds, UK, LS10 1LT;
  Royal Armouries, HM Tower of London, London, UK, EC3N 4AB

🌐 www.britarch.ac.uk/yac